BLOODAXE BOOKS

HGREEN, TARSET, NORTHUMBERLAND NE48 1RP

TELEPHONE: 01434-240500   FAX: 01434-240505

E-MAIL: publicity@bloodaxebooks.com

Please find enclosed a review / complimentary copy of

Anne Rouse: *The School of Night*

Publication date: Thursday 18 November 2004

£7.95 paperback   64 pp   ISBN: 1 85224 605 7

FOR FURTHER INFORMATION PLEASE CONTACT CHRISTINE MACGREGOR AT BLOODAXE

We would appreciate a copy of any review or mention you might give this book.

Anne Rouse was born in Washington, DC, and grew up in Virginia. After reading History at the University of London, she worked as a nurse and the director of a mental health charity. Since becoming a freelance writer, she has had many residencies, including a visiting fellowship at the University of Glasgow. She has published three collections with Bloodaxe, *Sunset Grill* (1993) and *Timing* (1997) – both Poetry Book Society Recommendations – and *The School of Night* (2004). She reads a selection of poems from all these books on *Poetry Quartets 9* (British Council/Bloodaxe Books, 2004).

ANNE ROUSE

The School
of Night

BLOODAXE BOOKS

ISBN: 1 85224 605 7

First published 2004 by
Bloodaxe Books Ltd,
Highgreen,
Tarset,
Northumberland NE48 1RP.

www.bloodaxebooks.com
For further information about Bloodaxe titles
please visit our website or write to
the above address for a catalogue.

Bloodaxe Books Ltd acknowledges
the financial assistance of
Arts Council England, North East.

Cover printing by J. Thomson Colour Printers Ltd, Glasgow.

Printed in Great Britain by
Bell & Bain Limited, Glasgow, Scotland.

For my father,
William Dashiell Rouse

ACKNOWLEDGEMENTS

Acknowledgements are due to the editors of the following publications in which some of these poems first appeared: *Gargoyle*, *Mslexia*, *New Blood* (Bloodaxe Books, 1999), *Poetry London*, *Poetry Review*, *The Printer's Devil*, *Rising*, *Six Seasons Review* (Bangladesh) and *The Wolf*. 'The Elements' and 'Things' first appeared in *Poetry* (Chicago). 'Move' and 'Glass' were set to music by the composer Morgan Hayes as part of a song cycle entitled 'No Glints In It', published by Stainer & Bell. 'Sighting' and 'Mrs Hues' were included on *Poetry Quartets: 9* (British Council/Bloodaxe Books, 2004) together with poems from other books.

The Year 1 Drama students at the Royal Scottish Academy of Music and Drama, Glasgow, directed by Hilary Jones, performed some of these poems in May 2002. I'm grateful for their insightful comments.

I'm immensely indebted to the Royal Literary Fund under the chairmanship of Hilary Spurling, and especially to Steve Cook, for their timely and generous assistance. My sincere thanks also to the Poetry Café, the Poetry Society, Arts Council England, Collage Arts in Haringey, Liverpool Arts, the Hawthenden Trust and Benenden School for sponsoring writing residencies, as well as to former colleagues in the Teaching and Learning Service at Glasgow University and Jess York, John Bogart, and Phillip Chalinor for extensive practical support. Thanks to Irene and Bill Rouse, Mary and Ray Root, Elizabeth and Robert Brokamp, and K.D. Rouse for help from afar.

CONTENTS

The Elements

A small flame flings itself about,
a wittering, an astronaut,
riding the kindled air above
the burgundy chrysanthemum.

The flame, the red, the window view,
are the locus, fine netting for a haul
of happiness in a peopled room –
but mind is more than merely eye.

Mind is also fingers, primed
at once to manoeuvre, and move.
Include, then, that beat-up bicycle outside,
in the failing evening.

Sighting

Old, smiling man. Panama hat, cravat.
Saturday, town square, approaches
teenaged dad with infant in pushchair.

Old gives New the big hello,
and waving with a whole-arm motion,
suggests: a lifetime's arc, the globe,

the sun's diurnal course –
goodbye is in there, too – grandiloquent
as ceremonies of first and last should be.

Not with bluest baby-gro,
or gilt-edged card, or gaudiest baptism,
was ever better welcome given.

Cement Mixer

All afternoon,
I've been captive to its
nnnn – naa – nnnn,
the sound of toil.

Workaholic, dogged,
if it pauses for a minute,
its vitals whiten into rock:
it only rotates to sustain

the old sloppiness
of possibility; the jellyfish gleam.
Whether the form intended
is an overpass in Swindon

or the Glasgow School of Art,
a bollard or a sundial,
matters not. A dog's paw
might be as eligible

for attention. When it pours
it goes native, adapting itself.
That's the cunning.
That's the fly-trap,

care, and evasions
notwithstanding: permanency,
or what could pass for
permanency with us.

Twilight

Nettled, half-ablaze,
she stumped along shop windows.

It was either tat, or rosy come-ons,
and in the glass, the beetling selves
hissed, and multiplied.

At one end of the high road,
a sky like moleskin paled
to the colour of water.

She slowed, and stood
for nothing – mottled ambergris,
the smog's violet wash – a deepening

that went on, assuring with the mildest touch,
twilight, this is how it could be done.

Cattle Among Trees

Stolid curiosity inclines its head,
and ruffles its matted hide.
Life is grass. No lesser argument
intrudes. Cuyp's cows or Virgil's
would have stared as loftily,
tails casually fly-whisking
of their own accord.
Zen masters might grace the shade
with the same unpetty silence.
There's time for everything:
in the dusk, need
saunters slowly after need,
for movement, watering, shelter.
Jaws revolve, teats sag like bagpipes.
Panic will be as rare
as the stinging of hail.
'Alone' is a freak of the farmer's.
It's deceptive. It looks like eternity.
One, various Cow.

B Road

The feet learn its ways,
but the eye believes its huckster promises.

Potholes effortlessly shimmer, full of rain,
and the S-curve gleams, moon-white.

Oil stains and tarry crevices revert –
in this admiring light – to grey velvet.

Just here a man torched his bungalow:
two dead, the road won't even shrug as it passes.

Its macadam is ridged, and geological,
but fecklessly, like a thought,

it vanishes into a wood,
skims a low hill, flings itself

at the Channel, the violet offing.
Straight for France.

Fort DeWitt

Crack! It's the hour of parade
in Fort DeWitt's unblemished neighbourhood
of barbecues, and Safeway's opulent chill.

White-gloved soldiers file
in and out, and muscular recruits
pretend to die, at calisthenics.

Not a blade of grass awry,
not a scuff-mark. Behind the shutters
of the military post office, a rasping voice:

'If he thinks he can fire me
because some crazy woman in Panama
says I stole mail from a sack,

then he can shove it, he'll find out.'
And now the helicopter's stuttering descent;
the staid approach of horses.

Happy Hour

Three girls meander down Newington.
One commands thickly, *let the lady pass.*
They turn to consider me with incurious eyes.

They move off awry, like a pantomime horse.
The traffic croons home. Three rouged-up dolls
meditate hard and numbly at shop windows.

Whatever thrashes round in them, sleeps.
They totter on spikes, in frocks, amiably swearing,
down that leafy, singing lane.

Mole

A farmer beckoned on the roadside.
Wales, Christmas. I was an au pair.
I wound down the passenger's window
as a large, dead mole fell into my lap –
a fitting gift for the young aspirant,
although I didn't appreciate it then.

A role model, you might even say:
a night-eyed, tenacious tunnel-digger
at work in the sodden cold;
piling through regardless
of the rocks, and owls, and foxes,
and the farmer, laughing, by.

Old Footage

Empire Day. They arrive and arrive:
Boy Scouts, aldermen, Masons in stiff collars,
a thawed-out torrent of souls.
A veteran of Crimea dips and lurches across the lens –
lame armour-god, warning of us.

Brisk muslin girls sashay to the water,
and then we're in the dark. The piano falters,
the Errand Boy runs home, to a slum
behind the promenade. All's hushed, elusive:
black lilies, sirens in a zeppelin raid,

a khaki ghost shown waving from a train,
while the plot's left to hang, like the second storey
of a house that survived 1941,
with its bathtub exposed to the mist –
and our time begun, its furtive camera rolling.

The God at the Audition

A god attended the audition.
'Next!' the clerk bellowed; sighed.
'Deus, Max.' 'Role?' 'Anything that's human.

That last idle eon nearly did for me.
I fancy a change, a furrowed brow,
decades of stern responsibility.

I think it would be rather fun.'
'I wouldn't hold out hopes,' the clerk muttered.
'After all, it's television.

You might try panto.' The god was sore.
'In with the dames and ducks!
No, I want my full three-score

and ten, my *good* man,
angst, and bills, and dandruff, and some
unpardonable business with a woman,

ending up, theatrically speaking, dead.
Just one little meaty part, that's all.
I don't intend getting typecast,' he said.

The Fire Hills

I've laboured up the stone path
to the Fire Hills,
through black stream beds and gorse track,
overtaking a man with a nubbled stick,
and overtaken by sinewy fell runners.

The cliffs, the winking sea,
are old beyond enduring;
the flux makes me its momentary darling,
but I'm as they are, as old as they are,
hurrying towards other, and other.

Family at Dusk

Late – always late – and it's midwinter.
Now no one can read, in the near dark.
Car headlights are switched on to contain us,
and the church's emissary, in a blinking pool.
Someone is here before us, sixty years too soon.

A little huddle on a Virginia hillside,
weaving back through the upright stones
and the mottoes – Victorian, implacable –
we've had to catch up, but we've never been orderly,
and now, in a manner, we disperse.

But which silent group, which car? I guess
she can come with us, although she's rambunctious,
even for such unruly ones; today's she's a shambles
in her long scarves, with her mumbling suddenness:
a house guest, bohemian, grief.

West Hill

Portents in the east? Four pairs of magpies.
Dusk dawdles in from seawards, ring on ring.
The castle leers, a ragged wraith,
across the tumbled breathing in the grass
and prompts a sudden bellow from a man
whose prowling of the cliffs has been disturbed.
His avid protests sound too late:
the little guardian lights reassure along the front,
the town lights pulse below, and ascending, this
is where the great warm darkness is.

Move

It's not easy to walk the streets in this state.
A bleached blond guy holding hands with his boy love,
tells me to MOVE.

I remonstrate, I am moving, shadowed and thwarted
by the singular gravity of others.
(Cue for the screwing up of his face in exaggerated contempt.)

Well you may ask what brought this on.
Tonight it sings off me.
I'm bared to the pith, to the green quick.

Drunks, touts, and scamsters
approach, to introduce themselves
on wet curbstones.

Nocturne

Great aunts in wicker armchairs,
snow drifts, a pink 50s kitchen.
Throaty, Victorian triumph. *Gin!*
They were here all the time,

The old affections, they rise like bruises.
I lie face up on the bed.
Even the yellow dog we had
finds her way back, muddied, done in.

The tree in the alley dangles its claws
over the green, and ghostly blooms.
The sky, night-streaked and opaque,
turns outward to the ignorant distances.

House Clearing

Aunties, you're restless even now:
butterfly weed pricks at the Cadillac's chassis;
mice revel at tag, photos slide underfoot;
boxes heave and swell on the impassible backstairs,

as the haul of a lifetime is junked,
higher than Babylon, and its wiliest truths
begin to look stuffy,
compared with irrepressible you.

Already you've co-opted me –
even now, I've elected to visit,
scraping *billets-doux* from the porch floor –
brittle half-dust, with an odour of marigolds –

peering at the dun paisley carpet's
ambiguous soil, for its runes,
or its fleas, or its mulch of indifference
You have more forms than a hummingbird.

I see my baby mind bewildered,
clouding to take you in;
o loves my love extends
like a paper chain, in a cellar

crammed with the deferred and broken,
to bind your living gift –
with these arbitrary, unappeasable,
beginnings and ends.

Fire Tongs

I was down the oubliette once.
Couldn't see forward or back,
and slumped there, helpless.
Wait, misery said, wait,

and I saw, without light, a pair
of cast iron fire tongs,
and squatted, as blank as a beast,
in front of *fire tongs, fire tongs,*

until the mind ran up panting
through an unsensed door,
and I heard myself complain
of being caught between friend

and friend (intent on their
own causes, blind towards me),
as the dumb wood started
and sang out, a blue flame.

Glass

You clambered into that glass of whisky
as the station bar was about to shut –
the tables curiously leaning into each other
like mates in a photo; the shutters scraped down,
the broom and dustpan flourished
with French hilarity, like the barman's goodbyes –
after a string of comforts, whiskys, Guinness,
heading off to pied-à-terre lodgings in Richmond:
no need for the unremarkable courage of the Dutch,
no glints in it, you are loved.

Honours

Home late from a meeting where each of us
seemed to covet a badge, the kudos,
I came to a little archipelago
of chestnut husks on the pavement.

Stamped-on fragments, green cockleshells
in the arc-light's stain;
frayed slivers and cups that signified
the tree was coming into fruit.

Passing cars shuffled at the stillness.
The husks were scattered over the path
just anyhow, in that unyielding light,
but I'm claiming them, even so.

Tinnitus

It's hardly like losing an eye, you couldn't sue,
but one pundit reckons that silence is God; if so,
I'm godless, and nostalgic for the nights I listened
from the lair of the streets, to the starry window.

Instead what I learn and learn is a restlessness,
as supplanting the peace, a demonic sentinel leans
in the open arch of perception, whirring his barbed tail.
I get things done, like Sisyphus. Not even that.

Like some wan woman, washing her hair in the Styx.

A Right Pair

The gloves, due to be lost, have gone to their assignation,
sprawling on a Tube platform, or in a telephone kiosk,
aghast at the naked hands of the hired ladies;
murmuring of how they felt dirty, like serfs, I was in
and out at my own discretion. They'd lie
caressing my lap, or dangling from my grip like orphans.
Well, they knew I had a heart: they'd felt its obligato
tremoring at a wrist, but never quite benefited (or so
the woolly muttering went) but just see how they fare,
one ingesting the faint filth of shoes, tossed prone on the pavement;
its mate on a railing spike, skewed, saluting all comers.

Things

The dumb things, the laggard shoes and keys,
in the aftermath as the hall light
strafes the bedroom floor
through an opening door.

Out of a glutted backpack, these sure things,
witness to the body and its derelictions:
T-shirts snug as bedtime prayer,
socks plotting out their even destinations.

The useful things, so unintelligent
compared to the body's metropolitans –
the jazzy hormones and glib blood cells –
but faithful, so faithful.

To hand, foreswearing telephoned goodbyes,
meeting the skin unreservedly.
These things. It's not through them
that negation moves, this chill.

The Station

I heard a cry. Everyone did.
It rattled at the daytrip posters, the exit signs
in the station, in the bridal light of May.
I'm going to fall

A small boy walking, with a woman in tow.
She wore a grey mac,
that spelled out sensible, and plain,
but he'd borrowed fear from somewhere.

He couldn't stop. You could hear that.
The sound bodied upwards, into vacant air –
as if only the pigeons in the eaves
knew, and could answer.

Writer's Breviary

1 *With Strangers*

Disuse thickens the voice. This *here*
is a long step away from the natural,
from the creased snapshot of home,
and the reliable mate. It's a gamble.

It's vainglory, this plying for evanescence,
syntax like a murmurous twist in the gut –
not an actual sentence, nor for life,
but possibly a clause too far.

2 *Three Kinds of Making*

Sticks on a mossy bank connive
at the meanest of fences.
A crooked line ends with an apple blossom.
The maker has left no further trace of himself.

The farmer's hailing words in the leaf-gloom:
lit windows, extinct at midnight;
the whiteness of a page, as painted light.

3 *The Writer and Heraclitus*

Stand on its mossy ledges twice?
To stand here once is an endeavour.
Any certainty's been bartered for a song –
for less, tight runes, an insect discipline –
although overhead, a host of birds,
extempore, fearlessly call.

Chase

Lately the athletic gangsters and the beasts
of nightmare have fallen back
and let me run, aborigine,
pelting after the small game;

chasing a cygnet, last night,
the hard length of the road;
negotiating stacked boxes and bruised fruit,
for a bit of grey fluff that

evaded, tumbled soft, and when
I finally, peacably, closed my hand
I owned... a swatch of dust, as a cat slunk by,
knowing more than it pretended.

Curtains

The net curtains float suddenly,
once, twice, in breezy supplication:
now don't go yet, or *let's have a look at you!*
great aunt-like, and when there are no more
great aunts, their little ways seem precious.

That sound in the eaves of the loft, too –
a child imitating a ghost, steadily cooing,
or playing a recorder, badly –
imagination, this time, as a pleasured thing.
The wind as kindly.

Mrs Hues

Mounted on a fine bay gelding, dressed as a gentleman...
your money instantly, or you are a dead man...
Captured, Mrs Hues 'owned she was a woman',
thus admitting, my lord, that she had no business
with pistols, or a stranger's 200 guineas.
No business, certainly, with hanging. I present to you
Mrs Hues, not a girl on the razzle, a craver of thrills,
a vendeuse of nocturnal wares, but a bold heart, and a lover
of Mr Hues, who would sit by a guttering hearth
over a hot posset, and a copy of *The Vicar of Wakefield*,
awaiting the distant *tuppety tuppety* of hooves.

Aunt Sally

When she heard the proverb,
when they said, *old, gracefully,*
she thought they meant, 'still comely';
she didn't know that they meant, 'graceful in defeat'.

Renew, renew.
The body can't follow me.
She, addled with her loss, reneges continually.
I've loved, she said to the night, and the night said, *who.*

Behemoth

She approaches thunderously.
Her scaled heavy tail
sweeps, tick-tock,
over the boardwalk.

Sly, her piggy eyes
sidle across the gabbing crowd
who blanch and shrink, with ruined spears,
and touch themselves for luck.

Thinking of her, agog, in shock,
I remember trying for
a separate fate: scented and taper-slim,
a blonde unruffled flame at heart –

But now I know better,
having encountered her
in the shining puddles,
in the dregs of the glass.

She's not in a pew in a lark-wing hat.
She's not in the choir. She's not, she's not.
She's mutton fat,
a guttering torch, trailing black smoke.

Sum

Let's not revert to lovers' algebra:
if she, if you, if then, if I, if we.
You're hers, and that's the sum of it,
and I've held to a unique geometry
whereby the self's augmented, not diminished,
fitting its dramas to this little square –
and if no figure's perfect there,
it isn't for the want of application – and, like you,
I've risked a passionate miscalculation.

Lucifer, Baby

Lucifer, baby, you're in the dark age.
You're the woolly mammoth, music hall.
Evil these days, it's event, not presence,
no one guy gets to star, however screwball.

So Lucifer hangs about the studios
wearing black like iridescent scales,
and when he sees the dish, or doxy
of his dreams, sheds twenty years,
and fleet of foot, moves in,
as arch-controller, Lucifer-by-proxy.

His are the shadows dappling the canal,
the grip returning thunderbolts;
everything that's flung at him: his the slur
of treacle over answerphones;
night sweats, flies, and whisperings,
the skull in a builder's skip.

Lucifer consumes his lovers quite –
burnt match – and lays them down
between spavined brolly and bent ferrule,
spatchcocked, to hiss of mortal failures.
They go out pearly, lightened of themselves.
He drums them back to school.

Night drawing in, I stop for breath.
Look at the pink above the roofs!
Your lies are prettier than anybody's truths,
Lucifer – and what was that you said, again?

The Steps

She diminished the man.

She voodoo'd him.
Fear made her dream him
tiny, ant-like.

She dreamed she lost him
on the stair.
It would have taken him a year
to find his way up.

Each step would have loomed
like Annapurna.

Elated, at the top,
he'd have to face
the soft rucks and furls
of her clothes, strewn,
islanded in the hall.

He'd need to sling
his rope, one hair,
through the white plains of dust,
bridge a ravine
to the next floorboard,

and slay his fear
of that original woman,
face abutting the clouds.

Most of all, could he forgive
a final craning vision
of her, as monster,
monolith – before entering,

restored, as a man?

Tyrannosaurus

A dead calm among the giant ferns.
One windy premonition, whiff of gore,
then it's The Mouth,
cavern-jawed, with teeth like spikes.
Shadows dervish through the undergrowth.

So fearsome, to a fault,
can it be truly do-do'd? I think not.
I saw one once with the selfsame look,
with primal grin and ferocity
out of a nursery book.

Maybe when a straying comet blasted
those roughneck newts, the canniest survived,
havoc-ing on private ground of horror.
This one had gulped down its man-host,
and left for last a terrible, fawn's stare.

Baby Face

Hooded, softly insinuating terrors, he leans,
the pillowslip slips off his baby face.
Oh, it's you, the stealer, fist as big as an iron.
Yes, yes, yes, yes. I know what it can do.
Did I say I wasn't scared?
Can't you see my two hands trembling at my head?
That's me, old spoiler: shaken, but inspired

The Awkward Guest

I

The awkward guest cried *murder!*
into the round agog of the courtyard well.
A single self, a dark and distant girl,
rippled deep, as if to disappear...

II

The old house drew its luck from a mason's hen:
a pagan Tudor offering, sealed in a beam,
dry bones with beak agape.

In a trickle of days, the new wing went up,
navvies on Dexedrine, foreman grey,
Sir Jack's in London, back presently.

Meanwhile his wife picks quietly
between the stacks of dusty pine,
hiding her face in her hand.

She's eaten of a herb called *all-her-fault*,
and another called *heart's-fear*.
They can never build it big enough.

III

The guest could have sailed off
for the small ports that day,
of Penicuik, Dalkeith, Auchendinny –
returning, damp and bicycle-clipped,

with *Rob Roy*, or a Campbell tartan,
from the Heart Fund charity shop;
or a crystal shot glass, or a pine cone;
or a ginger man for tea.

But hers was the less explicable mission,
cold chronicler in a guest room,
a rag-tag of litter chasing itself down a rat-run
from Archway Tower, to station –

while outside a meadow gleamed with rain,
the white May Candlemas amassing
in glens, dells, blood-red sandstone crevices.
She worked on at her desk, alone.

The ghost of the Gothic peered in:
'Zounds! Leave off that detective trash!
Who needs another? I am venerable
and lonely. The bats attend me!'

A relic of the Real snorted,
'Oh, please, *your* acolytes are many,
if bloodless, and unsociable.
More difficult by far, to say what is.'

...but at that moment there were,
at once, actual footsteps
and a knock of doom,
and her hostess-fair, walked in.

IV

The lived *I* being above all, diffuse,
poised in the door of all its open rooms,
a rebus; an Egyptian eye, vase water –
to say *I vow*, is like kneading mist,
but there is another, tangible verb.

That afternoon, she watched it prove
agile, intent, as water bead, fleet
down the rim,
journeying to acknowledge the other.

45

Shadow Book

She made a shadow book, and put in it
taboo things: hungers, ancient fears
steeped in other fears, already black.
No pictures; words invariably opaque.
Edited by – to say, time, would be too pat.
Certainly the title page was blank.
As for readers, one would be too many.
She closed it tight. It floated crookedly
down the long stream, the opposite of Moses
in his basket, taking every *The End* with it.
It won't dissolve, or petrify, or open.
There are things like that. There need to be –
closed books, and dreamless sleep.

Survival

I find myself in a café-cum-
convenience store,
a pure oval of fluorescent calm,
when two toughs barge in, one handsome
but red-raw; the other pale, and thin.

I know them from the dream before,
wherein we had a brawl.
I'd forgotten it. They don't like that.
Don't worry, they say, one fine night
we'll get you going home.

I'm not worried, me. Hardly.
I shrink into a single nub of fear:
wince, and blur, and need to talk –
but the waitresses, with a certain smile,
lay a kindly hand upon each arm,

And before I can blurt out three
scared syllables, with one voice
they suggest that I seek medical advice –
and resume their chat of latest loves...
and this, too, is as it should be, only true to life.

Wolf

The lawns were silver, and every blade
and fencepost hailed the sun.
The wolf was walking her home.

Late in a bar crowded thick with mischance,
he'd scouted out for anybody free.
First one out the Ladies.

His furry, heated breath brooked no evasions.
He escorted her towards the shuttered day,
encircling her with one sure arm.

Out past the roundabout – for which she thanked him,
and shrank to a mote in his yellow eyes.
It was nothing, the eyes said, personal.

Nor was it for her, when she turned to go.
And then it was – personal,
running and howling, behind her.

Andromeda

Back from Andromeda,
the pilot goes to bed,
vacating the darkened cockpit,
the scuffed walnut console
of wartime, low-lit,
as in the after-hours of hospital wards.

At dawn the steel beast
lands itself, yawns, and ejects
a lorry onto an unpaved road,
through woods hung with green
and silver globes; met
by a leanness of wolves,

slipping greyly across tawny dust,
while the self navigates by Mars
as it sets, finally schooled
to be steady,
heartened by an old routine,
of coming back.

wings for wings' sake
discernible intent is
lured lone elipses whose
this ink-dense cursive cast by
as a human cranes to read
in the dead night to hector
the way that thunder will seem
signs and importunes
flexes and rears
as the collective animal
not for food or a mate
bull on an unseen tether
of pilings like a pointilliste
choreographed around the axis
fore this granular hastening un
clamations without why or where
pupil or arise as thick as a mob's ex
to blink and contract like the eye's stung
inaudible cyclone monochrome fireworks
up as flecks of soil start from the loambed
black in their thousands stir and fling themselves
Starlings lift into the air above West Pier

Awake

Awake. Awake, and unscathed,
if one day closer to the grave.
Warm in the hollow sleep has made.

Yes, limbs are present [starfish move] all four,
and head still presides, mustier,
inclined to doze, but chiefly, as before.

Over again, as if to scare
the invading light, a gull declares
endurance to the morning air.

Bracing for the ice-bath of the news,
already it's impertinent to praise
or hallelujiah, as if a night's survival was

due to a star, a guardian, a god.
Indecorous, when others died,
or watch, this morning, with the dead.

Aura

A winter sun is fingering the stalls,
slowly lightening, like milk in tea,
the plaster busts of Elvis,
Kowloon tartan scarves.

A vendor on the tarmac grips
a bag, shower-curtain thick.
His face, out of an abbatoir,
is garish with the cold, and now

there's company: a woman
rigid as a crane, an elder Fury
in descent, who angles fiercely for
a bargain lime-green double-pack,

as he rips, and splits the bag
into murky veils. Shadows fuse:
blunt animal, and flayed machine.
All this occurs in the no-time of a glance.

Behind them a granite sky is streaked
with fissures like a ruined plinth.
Their flurried moment lasts,
frozen with that long violence.

Seasonal

On the first morning, men turn their heads
at a tincture of blondeness, or the roll of a hip:
a pavement of them, swivelling at one accord.

By the third day the sky is brazening it out in turquoise,
and musical non sequiturs float through every transaction,
yes...so...and you?, smiling confidingly

as they punch a till, or guide a terrier across a railway bridge.
Suddenly, it's imperative to stroll down the parkland walk as a
       sonneteer,
imitating the blackbird with trills and sidelong cantatas.

Florentines

They drive to Rimini wearing shorts,
nibble at ungodly Yankee burgers;
lapse nightly in front of TV adverts for a 'flesh reducer'
in which nubile waists and thighs twitch hectically
under spidery electrodes.

It's no use. They lack our brutish aptitudes.
The ardent Tuscan spring breaks the mind like bread,
and out they swank to green promenades and cool piazzas,
where they're sacrificed, again, to the eyes
of the barbarians, seeking *bellezza, das Schöne, beauty.*

Outcome

Dawn shelter in the station waiting-room,
the spoils of night as dregs of tea,
the restless hand as porter's broom,
the Nile of touch as postcard of the sea.

The hurried voice as beating rain,
the driven breath as stubbed-out-on-the-floor,
the savaged clothes as orderly again.
The nerves' entente as thunder by the door.

Cliff Walking

When she strolls into town off the ridge
the long way, level with the peregrine falcon,
the shopkeepers shut tills and follow her out,
as if she's hiding their goods upon her person.

When she's said nothing in days and the animal stare
of the sea has dissolved into lights, and berries birthmark
her hands, and burs ornament the hems of her trousers,
there's a man who looks twice – and she wonders,

running the taps in the seafront Ladies,
if he's for her, but cliff walking has forgotten that stranger;
his quicksilver's anyhow one with the day's.
She leaves him to one who can sail with an anchor.

The Passage

In the passage between houses,
a rucksack gaped in the dirt, revealing
a milkpan, a toy kettle,
and a greenish, flat bottle of olive oil.

When I came up that narrow way again,
the rucksack was gone.
The cooking things lay absurd, under a wisteria.
I took the olive oil home.

The next time I climbed there,
the kettle had been kicked down
all 25 steps, and the milk pan
resembled a bopeep sunhat.

But today the passage undulates free
between the old-rose bricks,
the dark August leaves parting
for turrets, and captains' walks,

and a sliver of turquoise,
on which an immaculate sail
rides motionless, a small white yacht
whose invisible hull

winks, diamond, down the coast,
and what could it be signalling?
Never distress, the sea is too serene.
It must be the sun, its last late beam,

exiled, hailing, *goodbye*.

Plato Said

Strumming Parthian slave girls,
spikenard-drenched actors:
it's the glamour dismays me:
whining 'Achilles'
is a poor example to youth.
'Helen' won't keep Sparta
from nipping at the borders.

A lie is a lie is a lie,
except for the welfare of the state.
Your cave itself is metaphorical.
You covet glamour
for mere wisps of thought.
A rose is not capitalised.

It's the randomness that appals.
A farmer's stud chases
a young rhapsodist: soon,
every epode bears the image of a bull.
He sings *aroma* instead of *agatha*
(today he prefers the labial),
yet pretends to honeyed immortality...

And so we live –
Such are your versifiers.
And so we live,
in the shimmer on Aegea's water.

The Good Weekend

farewell the lads

Time to ogle the plaster rose, find a pub:
brass taps, and thumpety-thump in the jukebox.
Miss Muzak had swallowed a jackhammer.
What's that shite I yell above the heads
when an apparition rose like genie
exited from lamp, and towered there incarnate:
no helpful spirit, alas, full twenty stone,
and said, who are you calling shite?

Not you, I said. Not you.

London in twilight:
the pigeon-grey river,
Cleopatra's blackened needle,
a palette of greys,
low strands of light,
the first night of my weekend

Woke up – where – Earls Court hostel
via night bus – carousing with three Kiwis –
six to a room in iron bunks –
'continental breakfast', toast with jam.

Dolloping rain,
a grey wash between me and the city,
pelting, cold, urgent.

The Underground's flat breath.
Lulling, warmed –
the knowingness of trains.

King's Cross. An empty platform,
only a woman testing
the air with her white stick;
she hovers, stalls.

Have you got a cigarette, a light.

Don't smoke love.
Well someone's got a cigarette alight,
and they should PUT IT OUT.

Thirty-one climbed up
the escalator into flash-fire, their death
hurled at them.
At the top, white carnations lie
beneath the plaque.

Out at Piccadilly's
whirlygig of traffic,
Eros directing it.
Dart into lurid Soho sidestreets.
Ahhh –

On foot to Finsbury Park, afflicted
with hunger, thirst, and a thirst for women.
Bread, twenty-seven pence a budget loaf
from the late-night Tesco's,
water from the tap in the public bog,
and women eluding me,

and stand in the cheerful midnight street,
a rock in the stream off the night buses,

then kip down under billowing pink
rhododendrons
for a couple of cold hours.

And up, rigid,
to the smell of the black earth,
and skirting the fence to avoid the keepers,
and walking to warm myself.

Jesus will it be dawn.

Poring for coins in a backstreet gutter
a ginger cat nuzzling,
under the shut-eyed houses,

turn again –

turn again,

and sit athwart the pedestrian bridge, feet splayed, and watch
the slim blue spires of earliest morning;
eating the unadorned bread, and greet the northern wanderer
as it hurtles unstinting now and lit
with dawn that sleekly rides its black full-throttled heart of fury –

timely,
the 5:03.

Telegraph Pole

A telegraph pole rides prone
on a flatbed truck,
its periwig awry, the white
ceramic conductors twined with rust –
creosoted, splintered tree of knowledge,
draped with jackdaw litter, hung with talk.

It fell last night, in the gale,
and rides through burnished streets
to the lumber yard.

Black wires underscore the horizon.
Poles march over the reedbed,
rootless, and branchless.
Clamped horizontal to the lorry bed,
Ajax borne off on the field of Troy.

China Head

a version of pastoral

On the edge of a great estate,
I found a little china head,
staring up through the blue speedwell;
a straw-hatted boy, Italianate,
freckled with dirt.

The keeper's donkeys nudge the fence
another spring, and April's mud
breeds vetch, and campion.
The shepherd gazes out, at bloody births
and undistinguished deaths.

Secure now in the boggy earth,
with rootlings for a coverlet,
against tremors of the figurine,
as piquet players fled for breath
out to the flowery borders of a myth –

indignities of nature irk him less
than these, the fractious chatelaines
and weary planters – wan
as any Dresden shepherdess –
intoning hyacynthine verse,

while toilers raised the great gazebo,
the ha-ha, maze and parapet;
nameless, dug the lily ponds,
until language danced cotillion, slow,
if brightly, from the burned chateau.

If, beguiled by a general thaw, he ever
yearns to resurrect, he'll need his lines
reworked for him, democratised in fact; a bower
of vines against the April blast:
the deluge, now, blessing the wanderer.